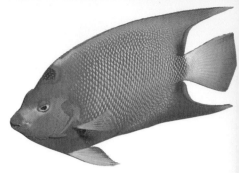

Photo credits

Dr. E.R. Degginger—Pages 7, 8, 17, 22, 26
Al Grotell—Pages 6, 9, 11, 14, 16, 18, 20, 24, 26
Kit Kittle—Pages 23, 24
Aaron Norman—Pages 25, 26, 27
Herb Segars—Page 7
Tom McHugh/Photo Researchers—Pages 18, 19
American Fisheries Society—Pages 6, 8, 10, 11, 14, 22, 23, 29
Stephen Frink/WaterHouse—Pages 7, 9, 10, 12-16, 19, 21, 24, 25, 28
Robert Holland/WaterHouse—Page 11
Rod & Kathy Canham/WaterHouse—Pages 13, 17, 21
Marty Snyderman/WaterHouse—Pages 14, 19, 29
Carl Roessler/WaterHouse—Pages 16, 20
Barbara Doernbach/WaterHouse—Page 28
Animals Animals—Front Cover
Stephen Frink/WaterHouse—End pages

Illustrations

Crystal Palette—Pages 7, 9, 10
Howard S. Friedman—Pages 8, 13, 22
Karen McKee—Pages 7, 8, 11, 15, 18, 21, 24, 25, 26, 28, 29

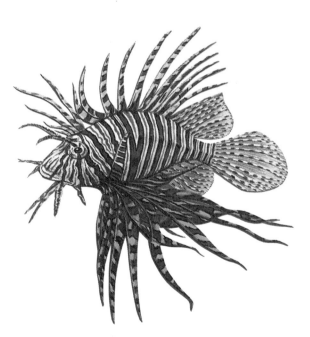

Copyright ©1993
Kidsbooks, Inc.
3535 West Peterson Ave.
Chicago, IL 60659

Manufactured in the United States of America

EYES ON NATURE™

FISH

Written by
Jane P. Resnick

kidsbooks®
Incorporated

FISH STORY

Water covers approximately 75% of the earth's surface. In it swim billions of fish from over 25,000 species. Fish are cold-blooded. Their blood temperature changes with the temperature of the surrounding water. Fish can live in a warm lake in summer and stay in that same ice-covered lake in winter.

Water Works

A fish is naturally equipped to live in water. It has gills for taking oxygen from the water, and a swim bladder, like a balloon, to keep it afloat. By changing the amount of air in its bladder, a fish never rises or sinks, but stays balanced.

Dorsal Fin

Pectoral Fin

Gill Cover

Breathing

A fish "breathes in" by passing water through its mouth. The gill covers close to keep the water in. Then the gills remove the oxygen and pass it into the bloodstream. To "breathe out," the mouth closes tightly and the gill covers open to let water out.

Armed With Scales

A fish's overlapping scales are called "armor" because they protect the fish. Mucous, a slimy substance, moistens the scales, protects them from infection, and helps the fish slip through the water faster.

Pelvic Fin

◀ Sensitive Nose

Fish have openings on their snouts that do the work of human nostrils. The paddlefish has a super-long snout armed with nerves and sense organs that detect food. When it's hungry, all the paddlefish has to do is follow its nose.

Functional Fins

Fins move the fish forward, steer it, and maintain balance. The pectoral and pelvic fins are used for balance, steering, and braking. The dorsal fin keeps the fish from rolling over and works along with the anal fin to act as a stabilizer. The tail fin provides power, thrusting the fish forward.

Crayfish

Starfish

Jellyfish

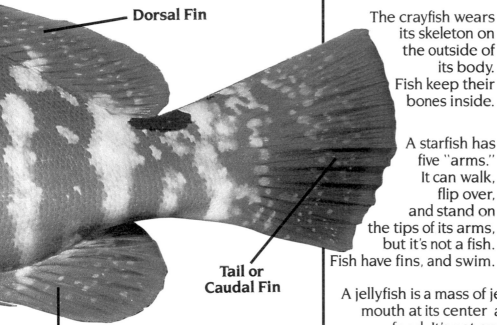

Dorsal Fin

Tail or Caudal Fin

Anal Fin

What's Called A Fish But Is Not A Fish?

The crayfish wears its skeleton on the outside of its body. Fish keep their bones inside.

A starfish has five "arms." It can walk, flip over, and stand on the tips of its arms, but it's not a fish. Fish have fins, and swim.

A jellyfish is a mass of jelly-like material with a mouth at its center and tentacles to gather food. It's not even close to being a fish!

Along the sides of a fish are the sense organs that help it swim around invisible objects in muddy water or keep perfect formations in a school.

Swimming In Style

To swim forward, fish sweep their bodies from side to side. The curve they make is a snake-like motion that goes from head to tail, with the tail giving the most kick. Some fish are faster than others, and the sailfish, who swims at about 60 miles an hour, is the speed demon of the sea.

WATER WAYS

Fish are the way they are because they live in the water. Water has given them their shape, their way of breathing, and their method of moving and feeding. But water has a variety of temperatures and currents, saltiness and freshness, shallows and depths, animal and plant life. Fish have adapted to these different environments. Some fish even live in pools that dry up for long periods of time. So as different as the water is, fish are different, too.

Fish Families

There are three basic types of fish.

Sea Lamprey

Jawless fish are hagfish and sea lampreys. They are primitive, snake-like, and scaleless. Their round mouths are like suction cups lined with more than 100 sharp teeth. This gruesome twosome stays alive by sucking the blood and body fluids out of other fish.

Sea Lamprey Mouth

Shark

Sharks, rays, and skates have skeletons made of **cartilage**, not bone. Your ears and the soft "bone" in your nose are made of cartilage.

The **bony** fish are all the rest, from a little guppy to a giant tuna. All these fish have a skeleton made of bone, the same as mammals, reptiles, and birds.

Guppy

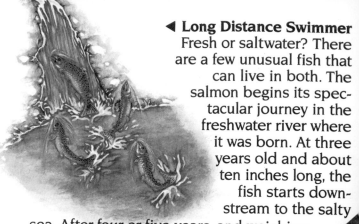

◀ **Long Distance Swimmer**
Fresh or saltwater? There are a few unusual fish that can live in both. The salmon begins its spectacular journey in the freshwater river where it was born. At three years old and about ten inches long, the fish starts downstream to the salty sea. After four or five years, and weighing up to 20 pounds, the salmon returns to spawn (lay its eggs) at the place where it was born. It struggles fiercely against the current, waterfalls, dams, and predators, arriving at its birthplace bruised and exhausted, but ready to reproduce.

Rock Bass

Yellow Perch

Sunfish

How Fresh!
Perch, trout, bass, and sunfish are the most common fish found in freshwater rivers and lakes.

Trout

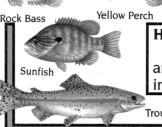
Viperfish

The saltwater seas are vast. But most fish live close to the shore where the water is less than 600 feet deep. In the ocean, the deeper the water, the dimmer the light. Many fish who live at 2,000 feet or deeper face the dark with light-producing cells called photophores. Blinking along in the blackness, the viperfish is equipped with the lights and teeth it needs to repel enemies or attract prey.

Whale Shark

▲ Meal Plan

The food chain refers to what animals eat. Big fish eat smaller ones and smaller ones eat tiny ones. The tiny ones eat plankton —microscopic plants and animals that drift in the currents in incredible numbers. Plankton, at the bottom of the food chain, is also eaten by the largest fish in the sea, the whale shark. This 50 foot, 40,000 pound giant doesn't eat other fish— only tons and tons of plankton.

Tropical Beauty ▶

Beauty may be only skin deep, but tropical fish have it. These fish live in warm waters among coral reefs, darting in and out of the coral to escape predators. They're small, swift, and decorated with stripes, spots, and colors that seem too beautiful to be true.

NAME THAT FISH

Fish have scientific names which place them in families so they can be studied in groups with similar characteristics. They also have common names. Here are some fish that have good reasons for their common names. They're funny, odd, peculiar, weird, and their names say it all.

▲ **Filefish**

Some fish are named for their shape, but the filefish is named for its skin. The skin of this fish is so hard and rough, it has been used as sandpaper — a useful fish!

▲ **Flathead**

The hammerhead shark has a head like a flattened bar — a hammer's head — with an eye and a nostril on each end. Other fish must wonder where the hammerhead is looking.

▲ **Triggerfish**

The triggerfish has a fin-shaped "trigger," and it actually works. The trigger is created by locking the spines of its dorsal fin. A frightened triggerfish dives into coral and uses its spine to anchor itself where enemies can't reach it. So to be safe, this fish has got to be quick on the trigger.

Can you guess why I'm called a unicorn fish?

◀Nasty Needles

Sawfish
is the perfect name for this member of the ray family.

Needle fish are silvery and skinny, and about six feet long. Slicing through the surface of the water, they look like, of course, needles. The needle fish uses its sharp teeth to snatch small fish and juggle them into a head-first position in its mouth. Then (slurp!) it swallows them whole.

With a nose that could clear a forest, what *else* could it be called? Its saw-like snout, about one-third the fish's length, has 24 to 32 teeth. In a 20 foot sawfish, the saw can be six feet long!

Cowfish ▼
The smallest creature to be called a cow has got to be the cowfish. Only one foot long, this fish got its name from the two cow-like horns that stick out of its head.

▲ Toothless Terror
The upper jaw of the swordfish grows and grows until it's a dangerous sword. A real slasher, the swordfish storms into a school of fish and rips its sword through whatever it can. Then, the eating begins ... but not the chewing. The mighty swordfish, who can drive its sword through a wooden boat, has no teeth.

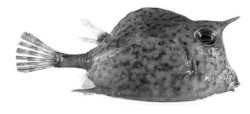

FISH DISGUISES

Fish don't play hide and seek. They hide to live and seek to eat. Nearly all fish hide from their enemies and some use disguises to prey on others. Color and shape are the most important parts of a fish's disguise. With all the fish in the sea, imagine how many colors and shapes there must be!

Seaweed Safety ▲
The sargassum fish is named for the seaweed it swims in. This is no wonder because the colors match perfectly. These tiny fish anchor themselves to the seaweed with "fingers" at the end of their fins. There they safely sit where no one can see them.

Ganging Up
Fish with bright stripes are not dressed up, they're disguised. When a big fish sees this school of grunts for example, all it sees are stripes, not heads or tails. If the grunts dart quickly in all directions, their enemy becomes even more confused—and finally, goes away hungry.

▲ Clear Sailing
The see-through body of this fish is so transparent that it's very difficult to see its shape. If it can't be seen, it can't be caught.

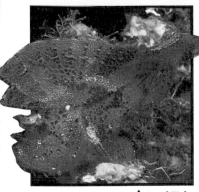

Lethal Disguises

▲ Leaf Fish

A leaf fish lurking among the leaves is practically unseen, while the frog fish is disguised to look like a piece of red coral. A smaller fish wouldn't even know these deadly predators were in town until (gulp!) it was too late.

▼ Frog Fish

▼ Spellbinder

This weird outfit belongs to the lionfish. Its enemies don't see a clear outline of the lion and don't know exactly what they are looking at. Little fish seem to be hypnotized by the spooky sight of the lionfish. They stay still and tremble, making them easy prey for a hungry lion.

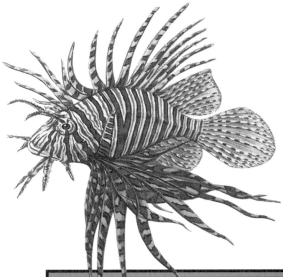

▲ The Eyes Have It

Some fish have false "eyespots" near their tails to fool predators. The eyespot is larger than the real eye, so the enemy thinks the fish is too big to eat, and that gives the butterfly fish a better chance of getting away — quick as a wink.

◀ Stoneface

A scorpion fish has a large, turned down mouth and warty growths all over its body. But being ugly is beautiful for the scorpion because it looks exactly like a rock with seaweed growing over it. All the scorpion fish has to do for dinner is open its mouth and wait for a fish to swim in.

Master of Disguise

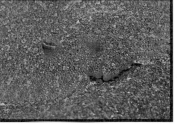

If you think you're looking at the ocean floor in these pictures, you better look again. What you're really seeing is a flounder, a flatfish that can change the color and pattern of its markings to look like the ground it lays on. These talented flounders can hide from their predators or remain unnoticed by their own prey.

SEA HORSES

The odd and beautiful sea horse has a head like a delicate horse, a grasping tail like a monkey, an outer skeleton like an insect, and a pouch like a kangaroo. With all these borrowed parts, the sea horse doesn't look like a real fish, or act much like a fish, either. Still, the tiny sea horse **is** a true fish.

Swimming Motion

A sea horse swims like the leader of a very dignified parade. Vibrating its barely noticeable fins like mad — as fast as 35 times a second — the sea horse seems to grandly glide by.

All Bones

The sea horse has bones inside *and* out. It has an inner skeleton like all bony fish — and an outer skeleton of bony plates. When a sea horse dies and dries out, its skeleton keeps its shape. People are so fascinated by the appearance of this odd fish, that dried sea horses are used in ornaments and jewelry.

Eyes Apart

The sea horse's eyes work independently of each other. One eye can look forward to see what's coming, while the other looks backward to see what's behind. It's hard to hide from a sea horse.

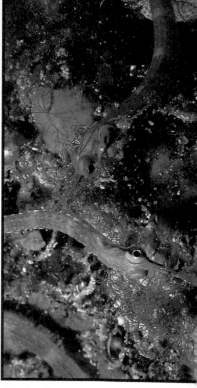

Stringbean ▲

A pipefish is not a sea horse that's been stretched or starved. It's just a skinny relative of the sea horse.

◀ Vacuum System

Whoosh! Click! The sea horse eats with its long tube-like snout which has a tiny trap door at the end. Whoosh! The snout vacuums up tiny forms of sea life. Click! The trap door closes. The sea horse may not have any teeth, but it does have a horse's appetite.

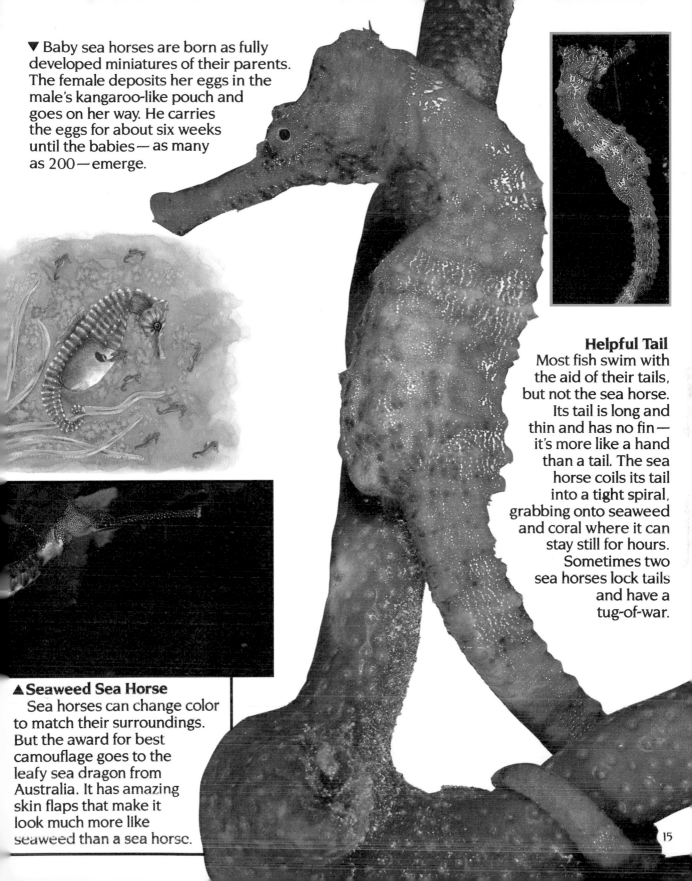

▼ Baby sea horses are born as fully developed miniatures of their parents. The female deposits her eggs in the male's kangaroo-like pouch and goes on her way. He carries the eggs for about six weeks until the babies — as many as 200 — emerge.

Helpful Tail
Most fish swim with the aid of their tails, but not the sea horse. Its tail is long and thin and has no fin — it's more like a hand than a tail. The sea horse coils its tail into a tight spiral, grabbing onto seaweed and coral where it can stay still for hours. Sometimes two sea horses lock tails and have a tug-of-war.

▲ Seaweed Sea Horse
Sea horses can change color to match their surroundings. But the award for best camouflage goes to the leafy sea dragon from Australia. It has amazing skin flaps that make it look much more like seaweed than a sea horse.

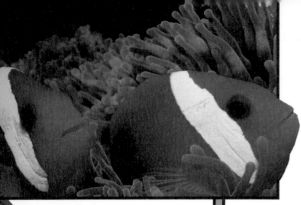

DEFENSE

Most fish are both hunted and hunter. That is, while they are searching for smaller fish to eat, someone is hoping to have **them** for dinner. How can a fish defend itself? Some have physical characteristics that put off their enemies. For example, no one is going to attack a fish with poisonous spines if they can help it. But, they may not know that until it's too late.

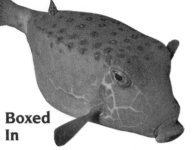

Boxed In

The blue box fish could be a turtle's cousin. It's covered with a tortoise-like shell except where its fins, eyes, and tail stick out. No bigger fish wants to take a bite out of this hard-head.

▲ The little clownfish lives among the stinging tentacles of the sea anemone, which looks like a plant, but is really an animal. The clownfish is immune to the anemone's sting, so swimming among the wavy arms of its friend, the clownfish is completely safe.

Sea Surgeon

Surgeon fish carry razor-sharp barbs at the base of their tails. These blades can be aimed —raised and pointed forward— so that a fish passing by can be slashed, sliced, or slit. As for people, the surgeon fish will gladly operate on anyone who grabs it by the tail.

Tough ▶ Puff

If attacked, a porcupine fish has a great defense. It's equipped with needle sharp spines all over its body, *and* it can swallow water or air to puff itself up into a prickly balloon. A big porcupine looks like a basketball spiked with nails. Now **that** would be tough to swallow.

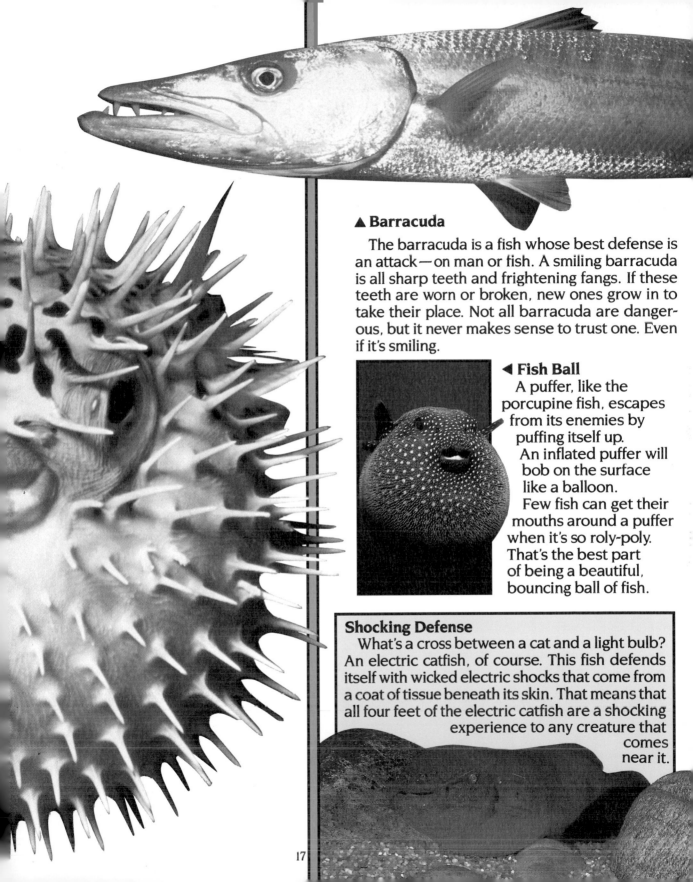

▲ Barracuda

The barracuda is a fish whose best defense is an attack—on man or fish. A smiling barracuda is all sharp teeth and frightening fangs. If these teeth are worn or broken, new ones grow in to take their place. Not all barracuda are dangerous, but it never makes sense to trust one. Even if it's smiling.

◄ Fish Ball

A puffer, like the porcupine fish, escapes from its enemies by puffing itself up.

An inflated puffer will bob on the surface like a balloon.

Few fish can get their mouths around a puffer when it's so roly-poly. That's the best part of being a beautiful, bouncing ball of fish.

Shocking Defense

What's a cross between a cat and a light bulb? An electric catfish, of course. This fish defends itself with wicked electric shocks that come from a coat of tissue beneath its skin. That means that all four feet of the electric catfish are a shocking experience to any creature that comes near it.

SHARKS!

Sharks have prowled the seas — practically unchanged — for more than 350 million years. These feared and fearless fish are different from "bony" fish. A shark's skeleton is made of soft material — cartilage, and its scales are like tiny sharp teeth, very rough and jagged.

There are over 300 different types of sharks ranging in size from the four to six inch spined pygmy to the mammoth whale shark. Some live in deep ocean waters, while others inhabit coral reefs or swim lazily above the seabeds.

Leopard Shark

Swimming For Life

Sharks are "swimming machines." They don't have swim bladders which keep other fish afloat. In order to keep from sinking, in order to live, the shark must swim and swim ... and swim.

The leopard shark is a long-distance traveler without even swimming. A champion survivor in captivity, this shark has traveled by air to aquariums all over the world.

▲ Blue Shark

Big Bite

Most sharks are carnivores, which means they eat flesh, mostly fish. A shark approaches its prey in circles, then bumps it with its snout. If it feels like food, it takes a bite. And that's no nibble. A shark's jaw has a force of 44,000 pounds per square inch! The blue shark's favorite meal is squid—lots of squid.

▲ White-Tipped Reef Sharks

Shy, white-tipped reef sharks are often found in groups browsing near the ocean bottom

▲ The thresher shark uses its ten foot tail—half its total length—to round-up and stun schools of small fish.

The carpet shark lives on the ocean floor and has a fringed head like a wig of weeds.

18 ▲ Carpet Shark

◄ Endless Teeth

Can you imagine a shark smiling! It would certainly have a toothy grin. Rows upon rows of teeth are set in gums, *not* in hard bone, so they fall out easily. However, lost teeth are constantly replaced by the ones behind them. Sharks can go through hundreds of sets of teeth in a lifetime. The size and shape of a shark's teeth depend on hows it hunts and what it eats.

▲ The nurse shark has flat, blunt teeth good for crushing the shellfish it finds on the ocean floor.

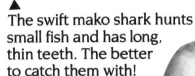

▲
The swift mako shark hunts small fish and has long, thin teeth. The better to catch them with!

▼ The great white shark has huge teeth — each a two and a half inch, razor-sharp triangle. It can sense the slighest vibration caused by a wounded fish. The great white also has an excellent sense of smell. It can detect one part of blood in 100 million parts of water — and even know which direction the smell is coming from.

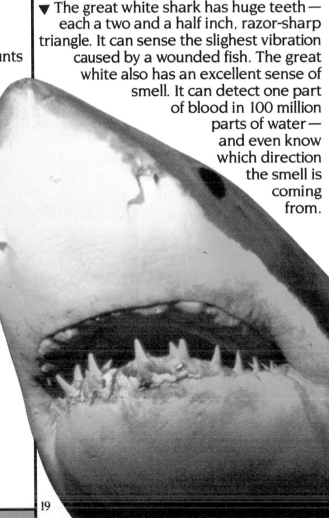

▲ The huge whale shark has tiny teeth — 3,000 of them. But this gentle giant only uses its teeth to filter plankton from the water.

RAYS

Cousins to the shark, rays look as if they had been run over by a sea-going steamroller. Their pectoral fins are enlarged and attached to their heads, forming wing-like shapes. When they wave their fins up and down, they move through water like huge, elegant birds. Like sharks, a ray's skeletal system is made of cartilage. Unlike sharks, rays are not aggressive — but they can be dangerous.

▼The eyes of a ray are on *top* of its head.
But the mouth and gills are on the *bottom*. To breathe, water comes in through two openings behind the eyes and goes out through the gills. The ray's eyesight is good and its nose, at the tip, is excellent. Its mouth is perfect for scooping up shellfish, crabs, and small fish on the ocean floor. So with this totally flattened, two-faced technique, the ray goes on its way quite well.

▲ **Spotted Skate**
Skates are members of the ray family. When they swim, they move their pectoral fins from front to back instead of "flapping" them like rays.

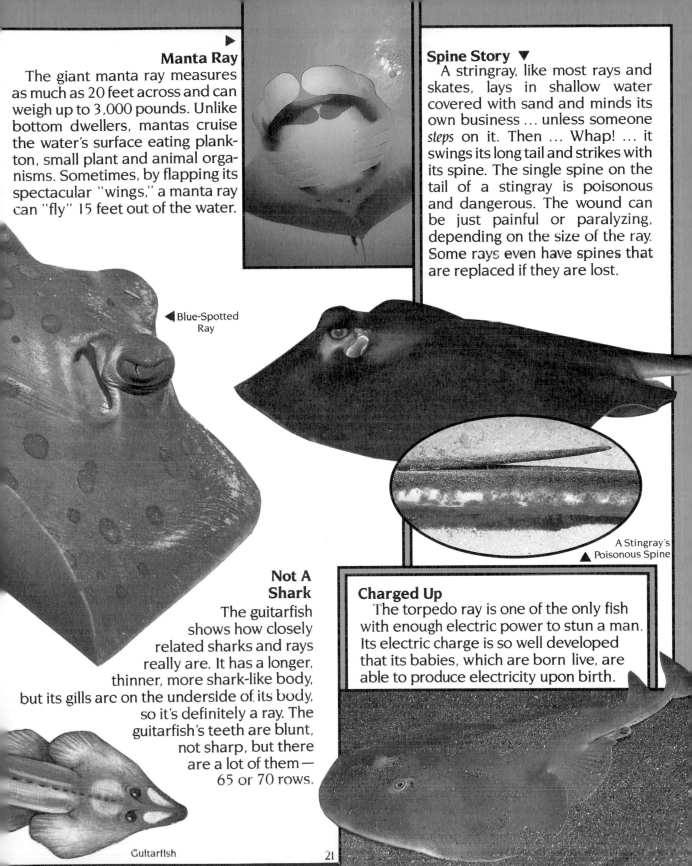

Manta Ray ▶

The giant manta ray measures as much as 20 feet across and can weigh up to 3,000 pounds. Unlike bottom dwellers, mantas cruise the water's surface eating plankton, small plant and animal organisms. Sometimes, by flapping its spectacular "wings," a manta ray can "fly" 15 feet out of the water.

◀ Blue-Spotted Ray

Spine Story ▼

A stringray, like most rays and skates, lays in shallow water covered with sand and minds its own business ... unless someone *steps* on it. Then ... Whap! ... it swings its long tail and strikes with its spine. The single spine on the tail of a stingray is poisonous and dangerous. The wound can be just painful or paralyzing, depending on the size of the ray. Some rays even have spines that are replaced if they are lost.

A Stingray's Poisonous Spine ▲

Not A Shark

The guitarfish shows how closely related sharks and rays really are. It has a longer, thinner, more shark-like body, but its gills are on the underside of its body, so it's definitely a ray. The guitarfish's teeth are blunt, not sharp, but there are a lot of them — 65 or 70 rows.

Charged Up

The torpedo ray is one of the only fish with enough electric power to stun a man. Its electric charge is so well developed that its babies, which are born live, are able to produce electricity upon birth.

Guitarfish

21

TRICKY FISH

Tricky fish! They walk. They talk. They breathe and fly. They even hibernate. Who are they and how did they get this way? Slowly. Six hundred million years is the age of the oldest fossil fish found so far. Over the centuries, as fish changed and adapted to their surroundings, some of them developed bizarre, fantastic behaviors.

▲ Walking Underwater

Watch a sea robin move along the ocean floor and it seems to be walking. Six rays, three from each pectoral fin, stick out and poke around in the sand. This trickster can even "talk." By vibrating its swim bladder, it can produce a croaking sound.

Fake Flyer ▶

Flying fish don't really fly, but they do get airborne. Swimming very fast, they thrust their upper bodies out of the water, spread their fins and glide above the water. They can fly fifty yards in three seconds at 35 miles per hour!

Walking On Land

The frog-faced mudskipper can breathe on land. It carries water in its gills and returns to the water now and then to fill up. On the ground, the mudskipper struts along with its pectoral fins and even leaps by pushing off with its tail.

Take Cover ▶

Here comes the archer fish squirting bullets. Insects are its prey and water is its weapon. Spotting a bug on a leaf, the archer gets in position, takes aim, and "shoots" drops of water at its victim. A sure shot at four feet, larger archer fish can propel water up to 12 feet.

▲ Drum Roll!

Underwater music gets its beat from the drumfish who vibrates its bladder to make the noise it's named for—a drumming sound —and it can be loud. A school of drums playing around a ship can keep a crew up all night!

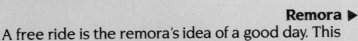

Remora ▶

A free ride is the remora's idea of a good day. This fish uses the powerful suction disk on top of its head to stick to other fish—preferably a shark. The suction of this two foot "shark sucker" is so strong that it has been known to lift 24 pounds. Now **that's** using its head!

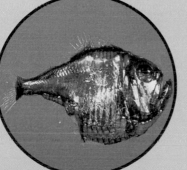

Body Work ▼

Fish get infections and parasites and fungi. So who do they call? The cleaners. Cleaner fish do the dirty work of nibbling away their hosts' pests, parasites, bacteria, and dead skin. Some work around the sharp teeth, and even down the throats of some very scary fellows. This moray eel stays neat and tidy with the help of its cleaner friends.

Flying Hatchet ▲

Meet the only true flyer among fish, the tiny three inch hatchet fish, shaped like a food chopper. Whizzing along for about six feet, flapping its pectoral fins like mad, this fish actually **flies!** Huge chest muscles, a quarter of its weight, give the hatchet the power to take off.

EELS

In ancient times people thought that eels were related to snakes and worms. Eels, however, are true fish with fins and gills and scales. Many swim in both salt and fresh water, something most fish can't do. The most common eels are anywhere from one and a half to six feet long and live in lakes, river bottoms, harbors, and marshes.

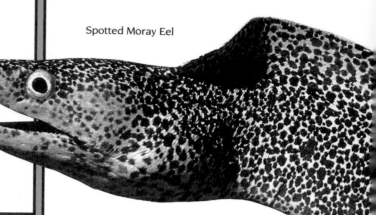
Spotted Moray Eel

Slippery As An Eel
Eels have more mucous than most fish.

Spotted Spoon-Nose Eel

That might make an eel feel good, but it makes touching one a pretty slimy experience. This spotted spoon-nose eel is one of about 600 species of eels.

Eel Garden
What looks like a question mark, lives in colonies, and acts like a real stick-in-the-mud? The garden eel. Garden eels spend all their time stuck tail-first in holes on the ocean floor. They rarely leave their burrows and if danger comes, they sink right in up to their eyeballs. As many as a thousand may live together.

Irritable Eel ▲
The "rattlesnake of the sea" is the moray eel, a fish that is as vicious as it looks. There are many types of morays hiding in the nooks and crannies of coral reefs. Some are large, reaching up to ten feet and weighing 200 pounds. And some are poisonous — as if strong jaws, sharp teeth, and a powerful bite weren't enough.

A moray eel will hide in anything it can fit into, even this tube sponge.

24

▲ The Shocking Truth

The electric eel is a six foot long fish that swims in the rivers of South America. Most of its body is filled with special battery-like organs. A short blast of its electricity can stun a man and paralyze or kill small prey.

▲ Trip Of A Lifetime

Anguilla eels, the most common freshwater eels, live in inland lakes and rivers. These eels migrate, sometimes thousands of miles, to lay their eggs in the Sargasso Sea, an area in the Atlantic Ocean thick with seaweed. The babies that are born return to the same place their parents came from. These baby eels will become adults living in freshwater who will again return to the Sargasso Sea to spawn. No one knows why.

This spotted moray lets a cleaner shrimp pick its teeth. ▼

Early Stages

1.
2.
3.

In its infancy, an eel is a tiny, leaf-shaped creature. In childhood it becomes a "glass eel," a little see-through eel. Then it changes into an "elver," a small, black eel, probably a teenager in eel life.

AND BABY MAKES 3,000

To reproduce, fish "spawn,"—the female places her eggs in the water, the male releases sperm and the eggs are fertilized. Most fish simply lay eggs and go on their way. But not all. Some build nests, dig pits, and find hiding places for their eggs. Eggs are good food for predators, but they are also the future for each fish species, so their survival is an important part of the fish story.

Not Clowning Around

This brightly colored clownfish guards its eggs near the safety provided by the sea anemone.

Surf and Birth ▲

The grunion rides the waves onto the beach. The female digs herself, tail first, into the soft, wet sand and lays her eggs. When she struggles free, the male fertilizes them. Then both wiggle toward the sea and catch a wave into deeper water. Two weeks later a high tide washes the eggs out. Two or three minutes in the water and the baby grunions are hatched and swimming on their own.

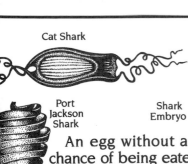

Cat Shark

Port Jackson Shark

Shark Embryo

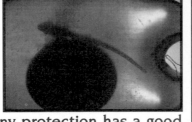

An egg without any protection has a good chance of being eaten. Some sharks and skates lay their eggs in leathery cases. Each one is the home of just one egg. The case has hooks that catch onto seaweed or anchor on the bottom of the ocean. There it sits for several months while the egg develops safely into a fish.

▲ Countless Cod

Fish that lay few eggs usually guard them, or none might survive. The cod can lay four million or more eggs a year, and the parents just let them float away without so much as a tail-wave goodbye. But only one baby in every million needs to live to continue the survival of this fish. If they all survived, the seas would be clogged with cod.

Safekeeping

Some fish search for a safe place for their eggs. The bitterling uses a place as safe as a bank vault—a mussel. To "deposit" her eggs in the mussel, the three-inch bitterling develops a tube. She uses the tube to place one or two eggs in a mussel and the male fertilizes them. Then the parent team moves on to another mussel, and another, making many safe deposits.

Toadfish Treasure ▼

Broken bottles, tin cans, boards, and plastic bottles—all these shouldn't be found on the ocean floor. But they are and the toadfish is glad. This fish thinks litter is an ideal nesting site. The male toadfish guards the nest ferociously. His treasure is hidden in the trash.

Egg Laying
◄ Champion

The ocean sunfish can measure 12 feet from top to bottom and weigh 3,000 pounds. It lays more eggs than any other fish— as many as 300 million eggs at a time!

Baby fish are called "fry." Although many fish have no interest in their newly hatched offspring, some do. They may just hover around to fight off attackers, or keep the fry in specially built nests, or even carry them around in their mouths.

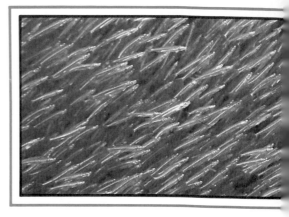

Under The Bull's Eye
Baby bullhead catfish have protective parents. The babies form a school and stay together. Like this mama bullhead catfish, the parents stay nearby and keep an eye on them until they're about two inches long — big enough to brave the world.

Mouth House
Tilapia babies hatch in their mother's mouth. The tiny fish may swim out now and then, but come right back when there's trouble. During this time, the "mouthbrooder," as this fish is called, gets pretty hungry. After a while, the fry may be safer on their own. If they swim back in, there's a good chance they could be swallowed!

Herring Hordes ▲
Silversides, as herring fry are called, hatch from sticky eggs that cling to stones, sand, and seaweed. Adult females, traveling in gigantic schools, lay their eggs at the same time, maybe 30,000 each. That's why there are so many herring in the world, one of the most numerous of all creatures with backbones.

The fry of this African jewelfish are ready to start life on their own.

28

F-R-Y

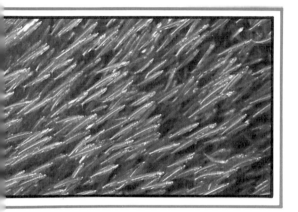

Bubble Nest ▶
The male siamese fighting fish builds a nest of bubbles on the water's surface. He carries each egg in his mouth and places it in the nest which constantly needs new bubbles. When the babies fall out and escape faster than he can return them, and there's no time to repair the nest, father knows his job is done.

▼ Angelfish
Newly hatched angelfish are stuck to their spawning place by a fine, sticky thread attached to their heads. If a baby does break free, a parent swoops down to put it back with the others. However, after about three or four days, the babies bust loose in bunches too large to lasso. Soon, the full grown angelfish are ready to raise fry of their own.

Babysitter
This fierce, male stickleback, two to four inches long, builds a nest for his fry and keeps them there. He tries to keep the babies from wandering off and may bring them back in his mouth. After about two weeks, the nest is worn out and so is dad.

▶ And The Winner Is…
Who gets the Mother and Father of the Sea Award? The discus fish, of course. These super parents don't have a minute to themselves because their babies are *attached* to them. For several days after they hatch, the little fish stick to their parents' bodies. This discus never has to worry about where its babies are.

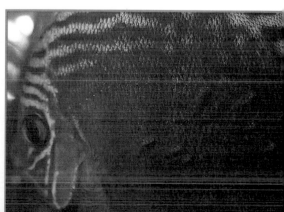